CUENTO DE LUZ

This collection of children's books, inspired by real stories, comes from the heart, and as a result of a collaboration between the What Really Matters Foundation, and the publisher Cuento de Luz.

We share the same dreams, the same hopes, and the same philosophy about spreading universal values.

We hope that families, schools, libraries, adults and children all around the world enjoy these books; that they are both inspired and moved by them, and discover, if they do not know it already, what really matters.

María Franco
What Really Matters Foundation
www.loquedeverdadimporta.org

Ana Eulate
Cuento de Luz
www.cuentodeluz.com

Pablo Pineda
Text © 2016 Alberto Bosch & Maria Sala
Illustrations © 2016 Silvia Álvarez
This edition © 2016 Cuento de Luz SL
Calle Claveles, 10 | Urb. Monteclaro | Pozuelo de Alarcón | 28223 | Madrid | Spain
www.cuentodeluz.com
Title in Spanish: Pablo Pineda
English translation by Jon Brokenbrow
ISBN: 978-84-16733-23-1
Printed in PRC by Shanghai Chenxi Printing Co., Ltd. August 2016, print number 1589-4

STONE PAPER

NO TREES · NO WATER · NO BLEACH

PABLO PINEDA

"Being different is a value."

Albert Bosch & María Sala

Illustrated by **Silvia Álvarez**

Today at school, our teacher told us a great story. We all listened very carefully, because it was about a real boy, with special abilities.

Come on everyone. Are you sitting comfortably? Then I'll begin.

One warm August day, a little boy was born in the city of Málaga in Spain. He was the Pineda family's fourth child, and they called him Pablo.

They were overjoyed with their new baby. He was happy, loving, and very peaceful, although there was something different about the shape of his eyes. They were different from his brothers'.

After a few months had gone by, Pablo´s parents were told that their son had Down Syndrome, a genetic alteration. It wasn't an easy thing to be told. They asked themselves what the future would hold, whether he would be able to look after himself, and whether he would have friends.

María Teresa, Pablo´s mother, would often cry to herself when she was alone with her little boy, until one day she decided she would never cry again. She wanted to concentrate on helping her son to get ahead as an independent person, without being overly protected, or without any limits to what he could achieve in life.

His father, Roque, taught him how to read and write
before he was five years old. So when Pablo went to school,
nobody would question his abilities.

Pablo´s first few years of life were marked by the happy, optimistic character of his family. It was a story of love and support for a little boy who they were convinced would have every opportunity in the world.

At first, the teachers were reluctant to accept a little boy like him, and they suggested that his parents should send him to a special education center. But María Teresa and Roque insisted, and finally Pablo was able to go to an ordinary school.

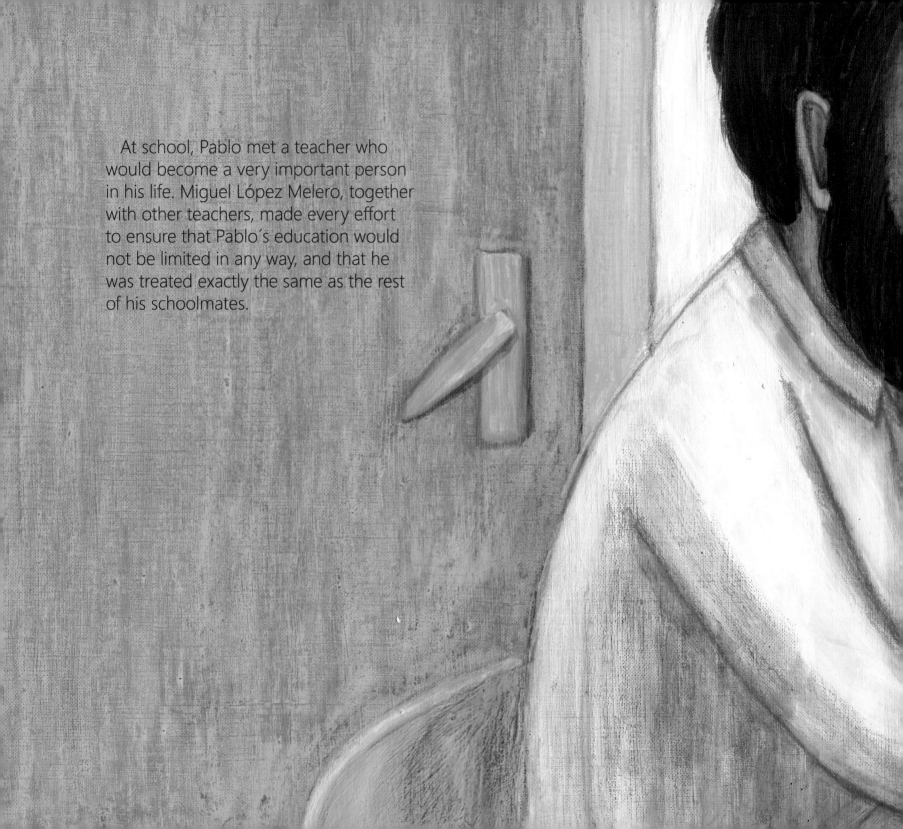

At school, Pablo met a teacher who would become a very important person in his life. Miguel López Melero, together with other teachers, made every effort to ensure that Pablo´s education would not be limited in any way, and that he was treated exactly the same as the rest of his schoolmates.

Pablo learned a lot, and they were years full of happiness.

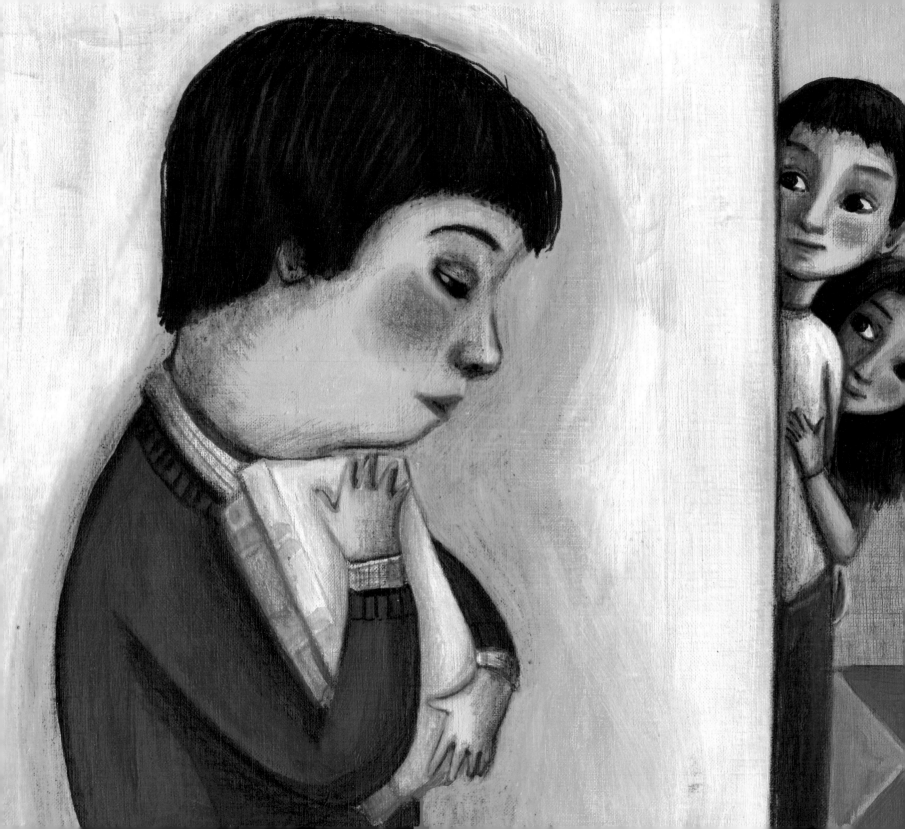

Pablo went to high school, and started to break down barriers. Nobody like him had ever made it this far in school before.

At first, it wasn't easy to get on with a whole bunch of teenagers, but thanks to his great sense of humor, they all became friends. Well, nearly all of them. Sometimes there were people who would say horrible things to him.

Pablo knew that he wasn't so different. He didn't like the idea of people being labeled, and he was quite sure that there were some things he couldn't do as well as most people. But there were other things he could do just as well, or even better, than lots of people! His heart told him he didn't have a disability or "special needs", just *special abilities*.

His graduation day was a particularly happy occasion. His family got a huge surprise when the director of the high school gave Pablo the prize for the best student in his year!

Pablo wanted to continue studying, and had decided to go to university. He knew that much of what he had achieved was thanks to his parents, and to having a positive attitude. He was completely motivated, and decided to study a degree in educational psychology, and to take a teaching diploma.

Studying a university degree was something quite out of the ordinary. Nobody had ever imagined that someone like Pablo would get so far. "The little boy with special abilities," as he like to call himself, didn't believe that anything was impossible, and simply achieved his goals.

This was also quite a difficult time in his life. He nearly always felt lonely, like he was being watched, ignored, and sometimes marginalized. But Pablo knew that all of these difficulties only made him stronger. They made him even more determined to work hard, and continue learning.

He was studying a degree, and showing how he could overcome difficulties. "While the world's getting ready, I'm getting ready too," thought Pablo.

And he did. He finished his degree, and became the first person in Europe with Down Syndrome to graduate from university!

The little boy who they hadn't wanted to accept at an ordinary school had made history.

All of the hours of love and conversations with his parents, all of the efforts he had made to learn in the same conditions as everyone else, had led him on to a new stage in his life. Now he was just another university graduate who had to face up to dealing with the adult world. His companion on this journey was his great friend, Fernando.

With all of his enthusiasm, his positive character and his desire to work, he was offered his first job at the City Hall offices in Málaga. But what motivated Pablo the most was being surrounded by people, especially children.

He loved reading and chatting, and he was very skilled at using language. His sensitive nature, his sense of humor, and his inquisitive, restless personality meant that he was quick to make friends with people. Soon he started giving talks in schools and at conferences.

This was how he began to take part in a series of events, where his opinion was greatly appreciated. The What Really Matters Foundation invited him to give a series of talks all over Spain.

Pablo's talks were a complete triumph, and he discovered his true calling. He became a wonderful communicator, capable of talking about a wide range of topics, but especially about respect, equality, dignity, and the rights of people with Down Syndrome. These people that have different abilities and not disabilities, as Pablo often says.

Pablo is always surprising others by showing new and different abilities, like his work as a writer. He published two books that were a great success: *The Challenge of Learning*, and *Children with Special Abilities: a Manual for Parents*.

Another surprise was his first appearance as an actor! Some directors decided to make a movie inspired by his life, and thought that it would be best if he played himself. He read the script, loved the idea, and with all of his usual energy, enthusiasm and courage, he accepted the challenge. The film, called *Me Too*, was a huge success, and Pablo even won the Best Actor Award at the San Sebastián Film Festival.

So many dreams fulfilled! But he has many more, like having a family of his own one day, and that in the near future, children with Down Syndrome will be considered as an example of how diversity can greatly enrich society.

The little boy with special abilities had become a university graduate, teacher, speaker, writer and actor.

Because he didn't believe in the impossible, he was able to conquer his dreams.

About the *What Really Matters Foundation*

The aim of the What Really Matters Foundation is to promote universal values in society. Its main project consists of the What Really Matters conferences, which are aimed at young people.

Every year, they are held in eight cities in Spain, and in another six countries. During the conferences, a series of speakers share the real and inspiring stories of their lives, which invite us to discover the things that are really important in life. Like the story in the book you're holding in your hands.

You can join us, hear more stories, and find out a little more about us at www.loquedeverdadimporta.org.

We look forward to your visit!

María Franco
What Really Matters Foundation